Fact Finders®

Kids' Translations

THE BILL OF RIGHTS

in Translation

What It Really Means

Revised Edition

by Amie Jane Leavitt

Consultant:
Philip Bigler
Director, The James Madison Center
James Madison University
Harrisonburg, Virginia

CAPSTONE PRESS
a capstone imprint

Fact Finders is published by Capstone Press,
1710 Roe Crest Drive, North Mankato, Minnesota 56003.
www.mycapstone.com

Copyright © 2009, 2016, 2018 by Capstone Press, a Capstone imprint. All rights reserved.
No part of this publication may be reproduced in whole or in part, or stored in a retrieval system, or transmitted in any form or by any means, electronic, mechanical, photocopying, recording, or otherwise, without written permission of the publisher.
For information regarding permission, write to Capstone Press,
1710 Roe Crest Drive, North Mankato, Minnesota 56003.

Library of Congress Cataloging-in-Publication Data

Names: Leavitt, Amie Jane, author.
Title: The bill of rights in translation : what it really means / By Amie Jane Leavitt.
Description: Revised edition. | North Mankato, Minnesota : Capstone Press, 2018. | Series: Fact finders. Kids' translations | Includes bibliographical references and index.
Identifiers: LCCN 2017015887 | ISBN 9781515791386 (library binding) | ISBN 9781515743354 (ebook pdf) | ISBN 9781515742180 (paperback)
Subjects: LCSH: United States. Constitution. 1st-10th Amendments—Juvenile literature. | Civil rights—United States—History—Juvenile literature. | Constitutional amendments—United States—History—Juvenile literature.
Classification: LCC KF4750 .L43 2018 | DDC 342.7308/5--dc23
LC record available at https://lccn.loc.gov/2017015887

Editorial Credits
Megan Schoeneberger, editor; Gene Bentdahl, set designer and illustrator; Wanda Winch, photo researcher

Photo Credits
Blue Earth County Sheriff's Office, Mankato, Minnesota, 11; Capstone Studio: Karon Dubke, (girl) Cover, top 7, (girl) 11, (girl) 28; Getty Images: Alex Wong, 25, Bettmann, bottom 23, GraphicaArtis, 20-21, Stock Montage, left 9; Granger, NYC, 14, bottom 7; iStockphoto: Eliza Snow, 5; Library of Congress: Prints and Photographs Division Washington, 16; Manhattan Rare Book Company, right 9; National Archives and Records Administration, background 4, 18, 19; North Wind Picture Archives, 6, 8, 10, 22; Shutterstock: Cafe Racer, (paper texture) 4, Everett - Art, top cover, 23, Joseph Sohm, left 4, Rafa Irusta, 12; Wikimedia: Lockal, (dollar) 17, US federal government, (coins) 17

Note: Essential content terms are **bold** and are defined at the bottom of the page where they first appear.

Printed in the United States of America.
112019 000110

Table of Contents

CHAPTER 1 *The Bill of Rights:* WHAT'S THE BIG DEAL? 4
CHAPTER 2 *The Bill of Rights:* WHAT IT MEANS 6
CHAPTER 3 *The Bill of Rights:*
THE STORY BEHIND THE BILL OF RIGHTS 20

TIME LINE 26
WHY DO I CARE? 28
TRANSLATION GUIDE 29
GLOSSARY 30
INTERNET SITES 31
READ MORE 31
INDEX 32

CHAPTER 1

The Bill of Rights

WHAT'S THE BIG DEAL?

Imagine having no rights. The government tells you what you can or can't say. You can't choose your religion. The government controls what newspapers and magazines print. If you complain, you get thrown into jail. You could be locked up for years without ever getting a trial.

Thanks to the Bill of Rights, Americans don't have to worry about losing their rights. The Bill of Rights is the first 10 **amendments** to the Constitution. These amendments list rights that belong to all Americans.

amendment — a change that is made to a law or constitution

The Bill of Rights protects citizens of the United States. You don't have to be wealthy or powerful. The Bill of Rights protects all citizens, even you.

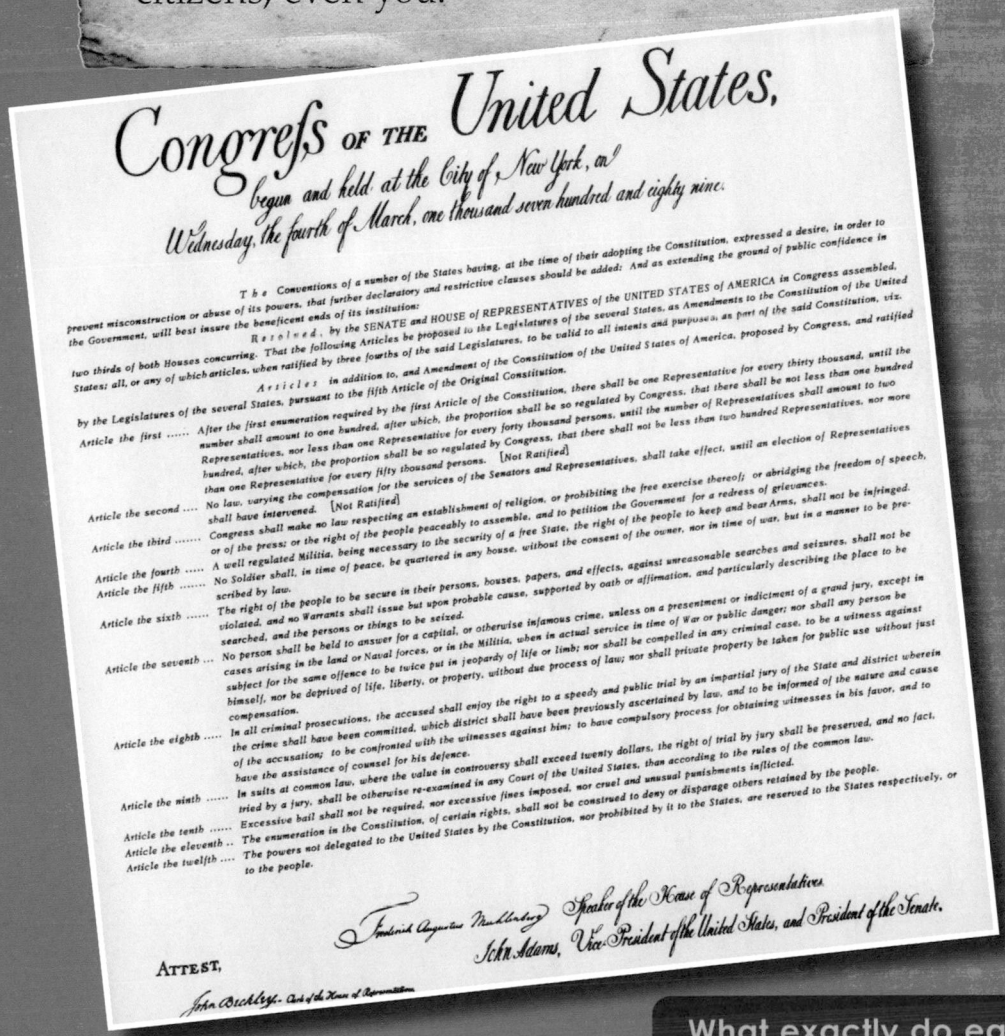

Congress of the United States,

begun and held at the City of New York, on Wednesday, the fourth of March, one thousand seven hundred and eighty nine.

The Conventions of a number of the States having, at the time of their adopting the Constitution, expressed a desire, in order to prevent misconstruction or abuse of its powers, that further declaratory and restrictive clauses should be added: And as extending the ground of public confidence in the Government, will best insure the beneficent ends of its institution:

Resolved, by the SENATE and HOUSE of REPRESENTATIVES of the UNITED STATES of AMERICA in Congress assembled, two thirds of both Houses concurring, That the following Articles be proposed to the Legislatures of the several States, as Amendments to the Constitution of the United States; all, or any of which articles, when ratified by three fourths of the said Legislatures, to be valid to all intents and purposes, as part of the said Constitution, viz.

Articles in addition to, and Amendment of the Constitution of the United States of America, proposed by Congress, and ratified by the Legislatures of the several States, pursuant to the fifth Article of the Original Constitution.

Article the first ..... After the first enumeration required by the first Article of the Constitution, there shall be one Representative for every thirty thousand, until the number shall amount to one hundred, after which, the proportion shall be so regulated by Congress, that there shall be not less than one hundred Representatives, nor less than one Representative for every forty thousand persons, until the number of Representatives shall amount to two hundred, after which, the proportion shall be so regulated by Congress, that there shall not be less than two hundred Representatives, nor more than one Representative for every fifty thousand persons. [Not Ratified]

Article the second .... No law, varying the compensation for the services of the Senators and Representatives, shall take effect, until an election of Representatives shall have intervened. [Not Ratified]

Article the third ..... Congress shall make no law respecting an establishment of religion, or prohibiting the free exercise thereof; or abridging the freedom of speech, or of the press; or the right of the people peaceably to assemble, and to petition the Government for a redress of grievances.

Article the fourth ..... A well regulated Militia, being necessary to the security of a free State, the right of the people to keep and bear Arms, shall not be infringed.

Article the fifth ..... No Soldier shall, in time of peace, be quartered in any house, without the consent of the owner, nor in time of war, but in a manner to be prescribed by law.

Article the sixth ..... The right of the people to be secure in their persons, houses, papers, and effects, against unreasonable searches and seizures, shall not be violated, and no Warrants shall issue but upon probable cause, supported by oath or affirmation, and particularly describing the place to be searched, and the persons or things to be seized.

Article the seventh ... No person shall be held to answer for a capital, or otherwise infamous crime, unless on a presentment or indictment of a grand jury, except in cases arising in the land or Naval forces, or in the Militia, when in actual service in time of War or public danger; nor shall any person be subject for the same offence to be twice put in jeopardy of life or limb; nor shall be compelled in any criminal case, to be a witness against himself, nor be deprived of life, liberty, or property, without due process of law; nor shall private property be taken for public use without just compensation.

Article the eighth ..... In all criminal prosecutions, the accused shall enjoy the right to a speedy and public trial by an impartial jury of the State and district wherein the crime shall have been committed, which district shall have been previously ascertained by law, and to be informed of the nature and cause of the accusation; to be confronted with the witnesses against him; to have compulsory process for obtaining witnesses in his favor, and to have the assistance of counsel for his defence.

Article the ninth ..... In suits at common law, where the value in controversy shall exceed twenty dollars, the right of trial by jury shall be preserved, and no fact, tried by a jury, shall be otherwise re-examined in any Court of the United States, than according to the rules of the common law.

Article the tenth ..... Excessive bail shall not be required, nor excessive fines imposed, nor cruel and unusual punishments inflicted.

Article the eleventh .. The enumeration in the Constitution, of certain rights, shall not be construed to deny or disparage others retained by the people.

Article the twelfth .... The powers not delegated to the United States by the Constitution, nor prohibited by it to the States, are reserved to the States respectively, or to the people.

Frederick Augustus Muhlenberg, Speaker of the House of Representatives.

John Adams, Vice-President of the United States, and President of the Senate.

ATTEST,

John Beckley, Clerk of the House of Representatives.

What exactly do each of these amendments mean to you? Turn to the next page to find out.

CHAPTER 2

The Bill of Rights
What It Means

The Bill of Rights
Amendment I

Congress shall make no law respecting an establishment of religion, or prohibiting the free exercise thereof; or abridging the freedom of speech, or of the press; or the right of the people peaceably to assemble, and to petition the Government for a redress of grievances.

In some other countries, the government tells the citizens what religion to follow. Many people have come to America to be able to worship as they please.
What?
First Amendment:
You can say or write just about anything you want. You can follow any religion you choose. People can gather in groups. And if you have complaints about the government, go ahead and speak up. The government can't stop you.
Before 1776, Great Britain ruled the 13 U.S. colonies. During that time, colonists could be thrown in jail for criticizing the government.
VIRGINIA GAZETTE
newspaper, 1795

The Bill of Rights Continued

Amendment II

A well regulated **Militia**, being necessary to the security of a free State, the right of the people to keep and bear Arms, shall not be **infringed**.

Amendment III

No Soldier shall, in time of peace be quartered in any house, without the consent of the Owner, nor in time of war, but in a manner to be prescribed by law.

infringed — taken away or lessened

militia — an armed force made up of citizens who are trained to fight but who are called to serve only in emergencies

What?

Second Amendment:

To protect the country, citizens sometimes must serve as **soldiers.** Citizens also have a right to protect themselves. The government can't stop people from owning guns.

Third Amendment:

Soldiers can't **barge in** and demand to live in your house and eat your food.

In the 13 colonies, militias were groups of citizens called minutemen. They were ordinary men trained and ready to fight at a minute's notice.

If British soldiers demanded it, colonists had to let them sleep in their beds and eat their food. This was called quartering soldiers.

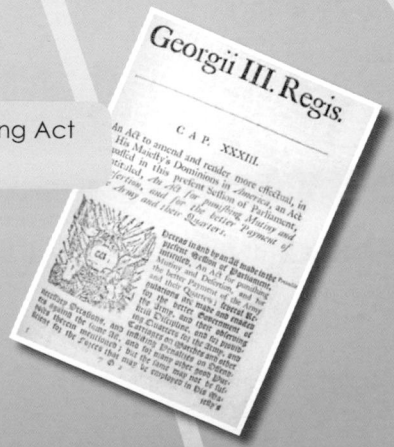

the Quartering Act of 1774

The Bill of Rights Continued

Amendment IV

The right of the people to be secure in their persons, houses, papers, and effects, against unreasonable searches and **seizures**, shall not be violated, and no Warrants shall issue, but upon **probable cause**, supported by Oath or affirmation, and particularly describing the place to be searched, and the persons or things to be seized.

probable cause — a reason that is likely to be true

seizure — the act of taking hold of or capturing somebody or something

What?

Fourth Amendment:

Police can't just walk into your house, search through your stuff, and take it away. First, they need to get a **search warrant.** And for that, they must give a really good reason for the search. They also have to say exactly where they want to search and what they are looking for.

Courts issue search warrants.

APPLICATION 1-1

COURT

STATE OF MINNESOTA, COUNTY OF

STATE OF MINNESOTA) SS.

COUNTY OF

APPLICATION FOR SEARCH WARRANT AND SUPPORTING AFFIDAVIT.

, being first duly sworn upon oath, hereby makes application to this Court for a warrant to search the hereinafter described, for the property and things hereinafter described.

Affiant knows the contents of this application and supporting affidavit, and the statements herein are true of his/her own knowledge, save as to such as are herein stated on information and belief, and as to those, he/she believes them to be true.

Affiant has good reason to believe, and does believe, that the following described property and things, to wit:

will be described as:

located in the of , County of , and State of Minnesota.

This Affiant applies for issuance of a search warrant upon the following grounds:

The Bill of Rights Continued

Amendment V

No person shall be held to answer for a capital, or otherwise infamous crime, unless on a presentment or indictment of a **Grand Jury**, except in cases arising in the land or naval forces, or in the Militia, when in actual service in time of War or public danger; nor shall any person be subject for the same offence to be twice put in jeopardy of life or limb; nor shall be compelled in any criminal case to be a witness against himself, nor be deprived of life, liberty, or property, without due process of law; nor shall private property be taken for public use, without just compensation.

grand jury — a group of people that meet to decide if there is enough evidence to try someone for a crime

Capital crimes are really serious crimes that could call for the death penalty.

A grand jury is a group of 12 to 23 citizens.

Fifth Amendment:

For a **capital crime**, a **grand jury** has to decide if there is enough evidence to charge you. You can be **charged only once** for a crime. If you are found not guilty, you can't be tried again. In court, you don't have to **say anything against yourself.** Nobody can take away your life, freedom, or belongings without giving you a fair trial first. And if the government takes any of your stuff, they have to pay you for it.

Being charged twice for the same crime is called "double jeopardy." The Bill of Rights makes double jeopardy illegal.

Choosing not to answer questions during your own trial is called "taking the fifth." This right is guaranteed by the Fifth Amendment.

The Bill of Rights Continued

Amendment VI

In all criminal prosecutions, the accused shall enjoy the right to a speedy and public trial, by an **impartial** jury of the State and district wherein the crime shall have been committed, which district shall have been previously ascertained by law, and to be informed of the nature and cause of the accusation; to be confronted with the witnesses against him; to have compulsory process for obtaining witnesses in his favor, and to have the Assistance of Counsel for his defense.

a jury trial in 1800

impartial — fair

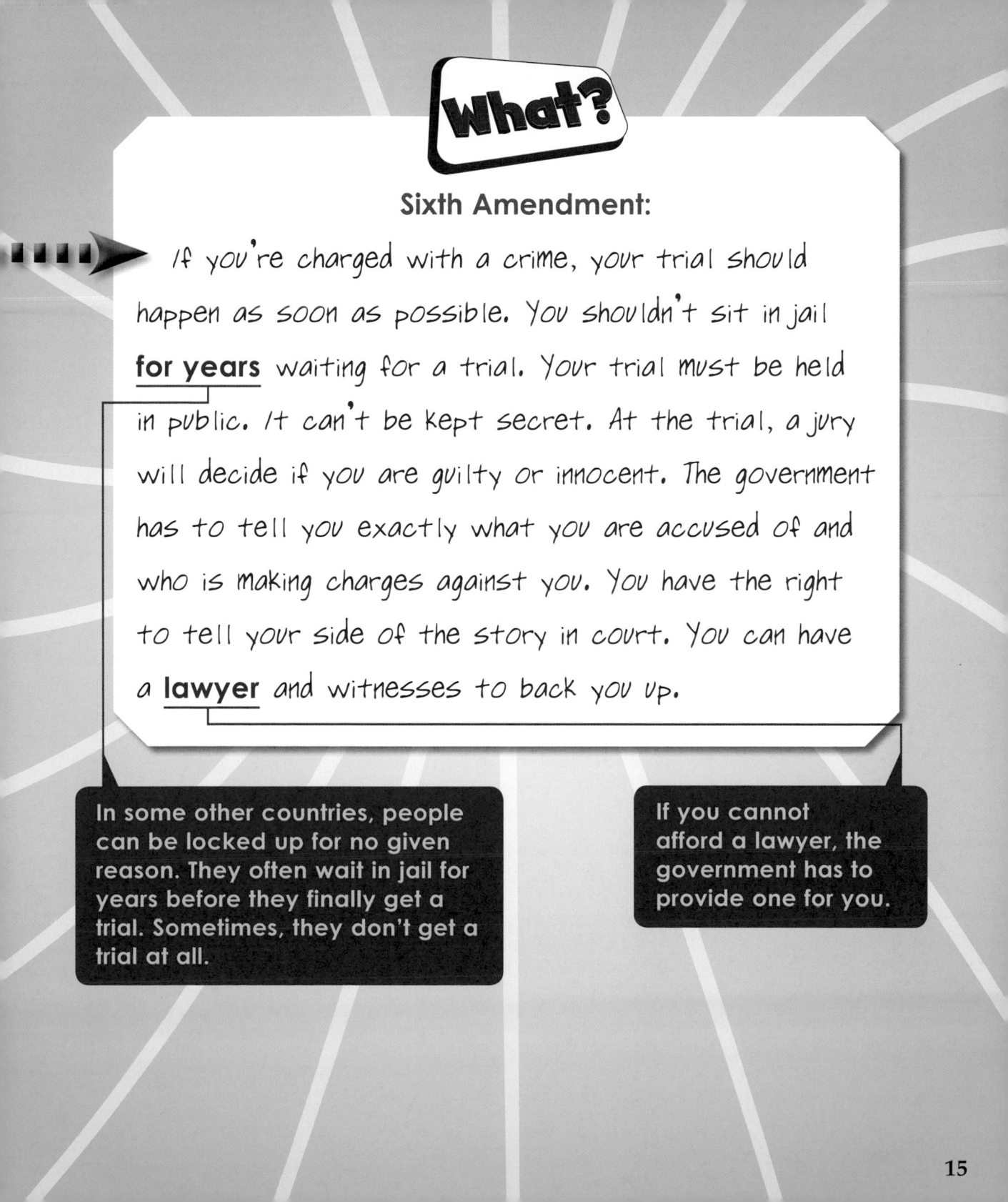

What?

Sixth Amendment:

If you're charged with a crime, your trial should happen as soon as possible. You shouldn't sit in jail **for years** waiting for a trial. Your trial must be held in public. It can't be kept secret. At the trial, a jury will decide if you are guilty or innocent. The government has to tell you exactly what you are accused of and who is making charges against you. You have the right to tell your side of the story in court. You can have a **lawyer** and witnesses to back you up.

In some other countries, people can be locked up for no given reason. They often wait in jail for years before they finally get a trial. Sometimes, they don't get a trial at all.

If you cannot afford a lawyer, the government has to provide one for you.

The Bill of Rights Continued

Amendment VII

In Suits at common law, where the value in controversy shall exceed twenty dollars, the right of trial by jury shall be preserved, and no fact tried by a jury, shall be otherwise re-examined in any Court of the United States, than according to the rules of the common law.

Amendment VIII

Excessive **bail** shall not be required, nor excessive fines imposed, nor cruel and unusual punishments inflicted.

bail — a fee you pay to get out of jail until your trial

Civil cases involve disputes over money or property, not crimes.

What?

Seventh Amendment:

You can have a jury settle **civil cases** involving **a lot of money.** Once the case is decided, it can't be brought up again in another court.

Eighth Amendment:

Your punishment should fit your crime. You shouldn't have to pay too much bail or unreasonable fines. The government can't punish you in a cruel or unusual way.

Back in 1791, $20 was a lot of money. The average person had to work 40 days to earn that much.

People shouldn't spend the rest of their lives in jail just for stealing bread from a store. If people speed in their car, they shouldn't get a $50,000 fine.

coins and bills from the late 1700s

The Bill of Rights Continued

Amendment IX

The enumeration in the Constitution, of certain rights, shall not be construed to deny or disparage others retained by the people.

Amendment X

The powers not delegated to the United States by the Constitution, nor prohibited by it to the States, are reserved to the States respectively, or to the people.

The Missing Amendments

The original draft of the Bill of Rights had 12 amendments. What happened to the two amendments that were not approved? One of them became the 27th amendment in 1992. It says that changes to lawmakers' pay can't take effect until after the next election. The second one has never been passed. It would have changed the size of the House of Representatives.

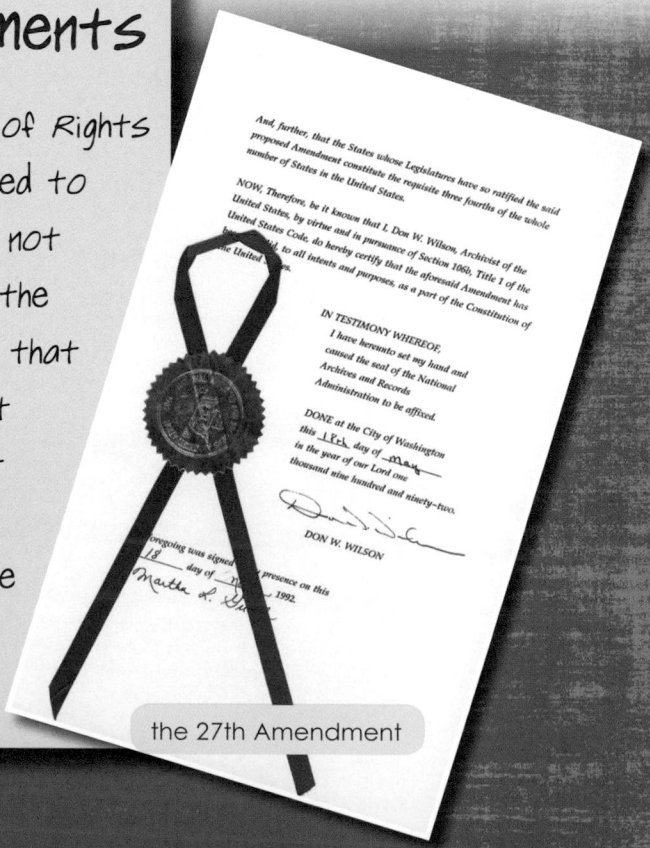

And, further, that the States whose Legislatures have so ratified the said proposed Amendment constitute the requisite three fourths of the whole number of States in the United States.

NOW, Therefore, be it known that I, Don W. Wilson, Archivist of the United States, by virtue and in pursuance of Section 106b, Title 1 of the United States Code, do hereby certify that the aforesaid Amendment has become valid to all intents and purposes, as a part of the Constitution of the United States.

IN TESTIMONY WHEREOF,
I have hereunto set my hand and caused the seal of the National Archives and Records Administration to be affixed.

DONE at the City of Washington this 18th day of May in the year of our Lord one thousand nine hundred and ninety-two.

DON W. WILSON

the 27th Amendment

What?

Ninth Amendment:

Just because we made this list doesn't mean these are the only rights you have. The government can't take away any rights from people, whether they're mentioned here or not.

Tenth Amendment:

What if the Constitution doesn't give a certain power to do something? As long as it doesn't say anywhere that the states can't do something, then the states have that power.

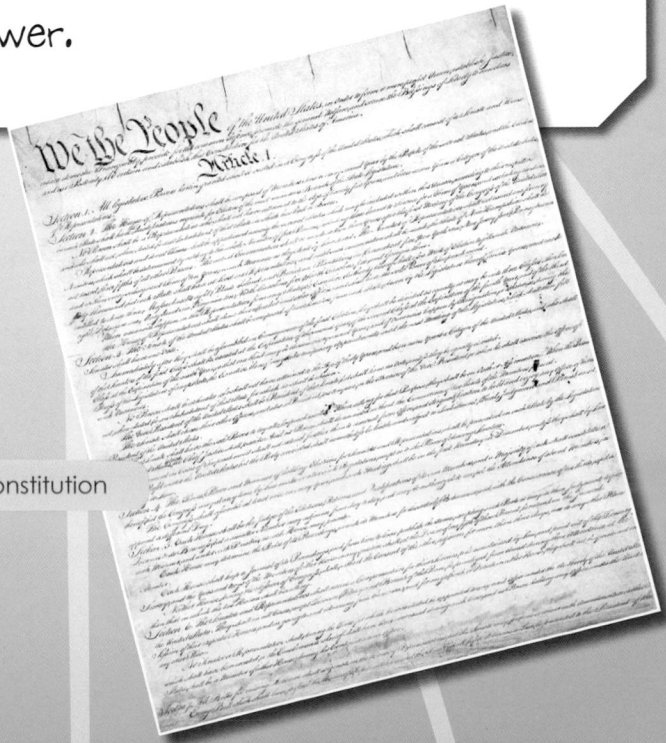

the U.S. Constitution

CHAPTER 3

The Bill of Rights

The Story Behind the Bill of Rights

Back when the United States was a new country, leaders from 12 of the 13 states got together. Their goal was to write a Constitution, a new set of laws for the country. Through the long, hot summer of 1787, the leaders argued about what to include in the Constitution.

the signing of the Constitution

Some leaders worried that the Constitution was missing something important. Sure, it explained the rights and responsibilities of the government. But the Constitution didn't say anything about the rights of the people. They wanted these rights to be part of the Constitution.

But even though they disagreed about some things, all but three of the leaders agreed on one thing. The country needed a stronger government. Both sides decided to sign the Constitution without a list of individual rights. They would deal with the rights issue later. On September 17, 1787, they signed the Constitution. Then they sent it to the states. They needed the approval of at least nine states before the Constitution became law.

The states held special conventions to discuss and vote on the Constitution. Two groups formed during this time. The Federalists did not think the Constitution needed a bill of rights. The Anti-Federalists disagreed.

By July 26, 1788, 11 states had approved the Constitution, making it law. But some of the states, such as Virginia, New York, and Massachusetts, wanted amendments to guarantee individual rights. They even offered lists of suggestions. And North Carolina and Rhode Island refused to approve the Constitution unless it was changed.

Crowds celebrated the approval of the Constitution.

James Madison

James Madison to the Rescue

The Federalists finally gave in. The people clearly wanted a bill of rights. When Congress met for the first time, James Madison from Virginia took charge. Madison looked at the lists of rights from the states. He used that information as he wrote his list.

Madison started with a list of 17 amendments. Throughout the summer of 1789, lawmakers discussed and argued about Madison's list. Finally, Congress approved 12 of the amendments. Now it was up to the states.

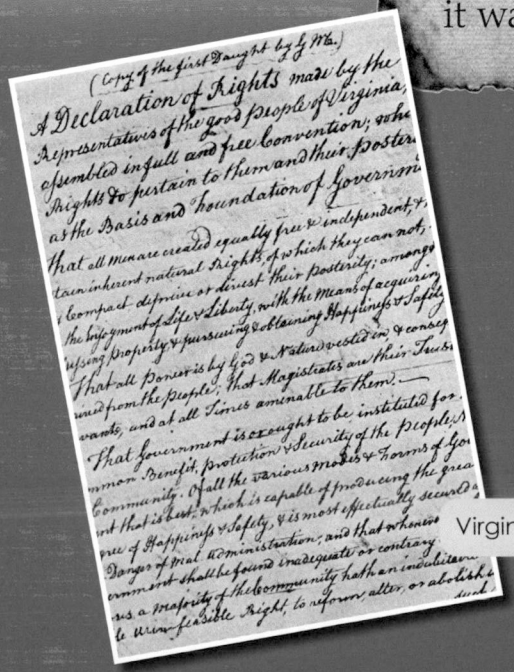

(Copy of the first Draught by G. M.)

A Declaration of Rights made by the Representatives of the good people of Virginia, assembled in full and free Convention; which Rights do pertain to them and their posterity, as the Basis and Foundation of Government.

That all men are created equally free & independent, & have certain inherent natural Rights, of which they can not, by compact, deprive or divest their posterity; among the Enjoyment of Life & Liberty, with the Means of acquiring possessing Property & pursuing & obtaining Happiness & Safety.

That all Power is by God & Nature vested in, & consequently derived from the People; that Magistrates are their Trustees & Servants, and at all Times amenable to them.

That Government is or ought to be instituted for the common Benefit, protection & Security of the People, Nation or Community. Of all the various Modes & Forms of Government that is best, which is capable of producing the greatest Degree of Happiness & Safety, & is most effectually secured against the Danger of Mal administration; and that whenever any Government shall be found inadequate or contrary to these purposes, a Majority of the Community hath an indubitable, unalienable & indefeasible Right, to reform, alter, or abolish it, in such Manner, as shall judge most conducive to the public Weal.

Virginia's Declaration of Rights

On November 20, 1789, New Jersey became the first state to approve the amendments. Virginia, the last, approved them on December 15, 1791. States approved 10 of the 12 amendments. These 10 amendments became known as the Bill of Rights.

Today, the original Bill of Rights is preserved and protected. You can visit the document at the National Archives in Washington, D.C. The Bill of Rights is displayed with the Declaration of Independence and the Constitution. Together, these documents are known as the Charters of Freedom.

The Bill of Rights is more than 200 years old. But the ideas it describes are still just as meaningful today. What was important then is still important today. And the Bill of Rights will always be here to protect your rights.

Saving History

The government goes to great lengths to save important documents like the Bill of Rights. Cases protecting the Charters of Freedom are made of thick glass. Inside the cases, special green lights shine on the documents. The green lights keep the documents from crumbling or fading.

The glass cases also have computers that monitor the building. If there is a fire, the computer automatically moves the documents to a fireproof vault 6 feet (1.8 meters) below ground. The vault is built with metal strong enough to withstand a bomb blast. Those are some well-protected pieces of paper, aren't they?

the Bill of Rights today

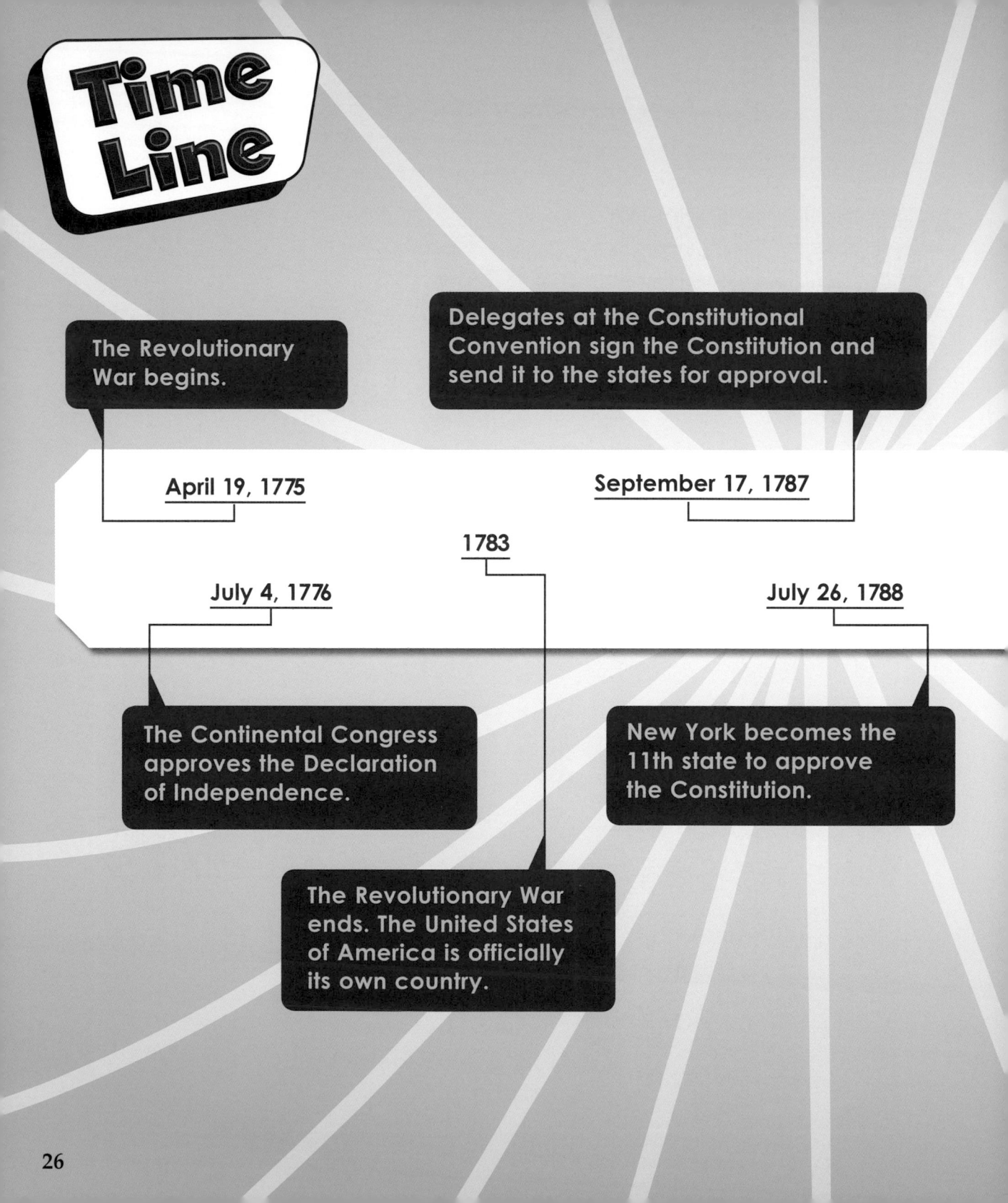
Time Line
The Revolutionary War begins.
Delegates at the Constitutional Convention sign the Constitution and send it to the states for approval.
April 19, 1775
September 17, 1787
1783
July 4, 1776
July 26, 1788
The Continental Congress approves the Declaration of Independence.
New York becomes the 11th state to approve the Constitution.
The Revolutionary War ends. The United States of America is officially its own country.

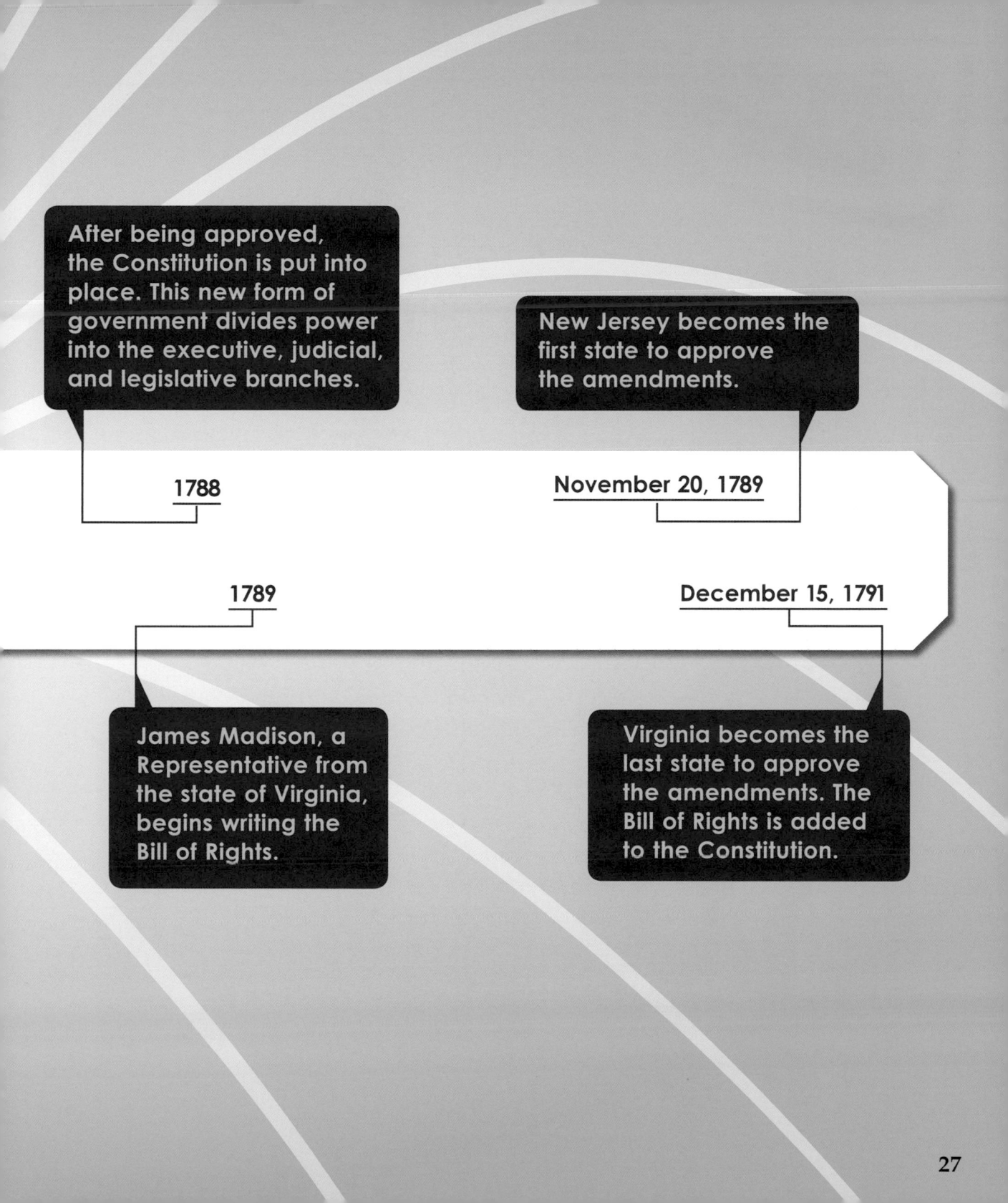
After being approved, the Constitution is put into place. This new form of government divides power into the executive, judicial, and legislative branches.
1788
New Jersey becomes the first state to approve the amendments.
November 20, 1789
1789
James Madison, a Representative from the state of Virginia, begins writing the Bill of Rights.
December 15, 1791
Virginia becomes the last state to approve the amendments. The Bill of Rights is added to the Constitution.

Why Do I Care?

Top Five Reasons to Care about the Bill of Rights

5. People can have different opinions, and that's okay. The Bill of Rights allows U.S. citizens to say what they think without fear of arrest.

4. We can get good ideas from everyone. James Madison looked at many different sources to get ideas for the Bill of Rights.

3. Change and improvement are important in life. The Bill of Rights improved the Constitution.

2. It's important to compromise. Even though the Federalists and the Anti-Federalists didn't always agree, they still worked together for the good of the people.

1. Governments need to look out for their citizens. The Bill of Rights made sure the rights of U.S. citizens would always be protected.

Translation Guide

bear arms – We're not talking about wearing sleeveless shirts. We're not even talking about having arms like a grizzly bear. In the Bill of Rights, to bear arms means to have weapons.

due process – Due process is not the process of checking out a book from the library. Due process is the established rules and steps in legal proceedings.

jeopardy – In addition to being the name of a popular game show, jeopardy means a risk or danger.

quarter – This has nothing to do with coins. To quarter soldiers means to give them a place to sleep and eat.

redress – Redress means to get dressed again. Just kidding! Redress means to help or fix a problem.

Glossary

amendment (uh-MEND-muhnt) — a change that is made to a law

bail (BAYL) — a sum of money paid to a court to allow someone accused of a crime to be set free until his or her trial

grand jury (GRAND JU-ree) — a group of people that meet to decide if there is enough evidence to try someone for a crime

impartial (im-PAR-shuhl) — fair and not favoring one person or point of view over another

infringe (in-FRINJ) — to take away little by little

militia (muh-LISH-uh) — a group of citizens who are trained to fight, but who only serve in an emergency; today, the National Guard serves as the militia for the United States.

probable cause (PROB-uh-buhl KAWZ) — a really good reason for believing that someone should be charged with a crime

seizure (SEE-zhur) — the act of taking something away from someone

Internet Sites

Use FactHound to find Internet sites related to this book.

Visit **www.facthound.com**

Just type in **9781515791386** and go.

Read More

Cahill, Byron. *Freedom of Speech and Expression.* The Four Freedoms. Minneapolis: Lerner Publishing, 2014.

Kawa, Katie. *Bill of Rights.* Documents of American Democracy. New York: Rosen Publishing, 2017.

Wolfe, James, and Nancy L. Stair. *Understanding the Bill of Rights.* Berkeley Heights, N.J.: Enslow Publishers, 2016.

Index

amendments, 4, 5, 6–19, 23, 24, 27
Anti-Federalists, 22, 28

Bill of Rights
    approval of, 23, 24
    need for, 21, 22
    protection of, 25
    writing of, 23, 27, 28

Charters of Freedom, 24, 25
civil cases, 17
colonists, 7, 9
Constitutional Convention, 20–21, 26
crimes, 12, 13, 16, 17

double jeopardy, 12, 13

Federalists, 22, 23, 28
freedom of religion, 6, 7
freedom of speech, 6, 7, 28
freedom of the press, 6, 7

Great Britain, 7

juries, 12–15, 16–17

Madison, James, 23, 27, 28
minutemen, 9

probable cause, 10

quartering, 8, 9, 29

rights, 4–5, 6, 8–9, 10, 14–15, 16, 18–19, 21–24, 28

search warrants, 10, 11
seizures, 10, 11
soldiers, 8, 9

trials, 4, 13, 14, 15

unapproved amendments, 18
U.S. Constitution, 4, 18–19, 20–22, 24, 26–27, 28